791.43
Sim

Simon, Seymour

Mad scientists, weird doctors, & time
 travelers in movies, TV, & books

DATE DUE		
APR 26 1983		
APR 30 1984		
NOV 09 1992		
3-21-05		

Mad Scientists,

Weird Doctors,

& Time Travelers

in Movies, TV,

& Books

Other Books By Seymour Simon

Mad Scientists, Weird Doctors, & Time Travelers in Movies, TV, & Books

by Seymour Simon

J.B. Lippincott   New York

SALK JR. HIGH MEDIA CENTER
ELK RIVER, MN 55330

Most of the photos in this book come from the author's collection;
additional pictures were provided by *Movie Star News.*

Mad Scientists, Weird Doctors, and Time Travelers
In Movies, TV, and Books
Copyright © 1981 by Seymour Simon
For information address J. B. Lippincott Junior Books, 10 East 53rd Street,
New York, N. Y. 10022. Published simultaneously in Canada by
Fitzhenry & Whiteside Limited, Toronto.

Library of Congress Cataloging in Publication Data
Simon, Seymour.
    Mad scientists, weird doctors, and time
travelers in movies, TV, and books.
    Includes index.
    SUMMARY: Surveys creatures with strange
powers, including those mysteriously transformed
humans that have appeared in books, movies, and
television.
    1. Monsters in mass media—Juvenile
literature. [1. Monsters in mass media] I.
Title.
P96.M6S48 1981 791.43′09′09375 80-8724
ISBN 0-397-31932-0
ISBN 0-397-31933-9 (lib. bdg.)

1 2 3 4 5 6 7 8 9 10
First Edition

Contents

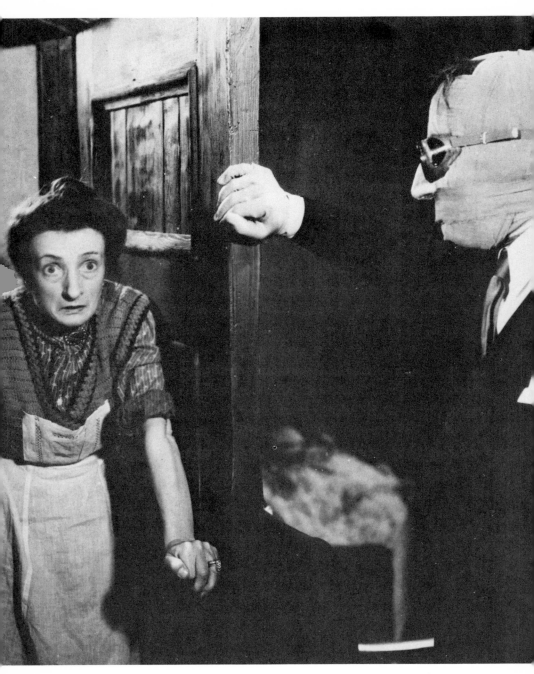

The Invisible Man, 1933. Courtesy of Universal.

1. The Invisible Man

A mysterious stranger appears one day in a small village in England. He is wearing a heavy overcoat. His face is completely wrapped in bandages. His nose is hidden behind a small shield. Dark glasses cover his eyes and gloves cover his hands.

The villagers are filled with curiosity. Was the stranger in some kind of horrible accident, they wonder. Beneath the bandages does his face show terrible scars? Are the bandages just a disguise?

The stranger makes no attempt to satisfy their curiosity. He takes a room at a local inn. For several days, the stranger remains in his room and has food and drink sent up to him. Behind a locked door, he experiments with chemicals. He only wants to be left alone.

But that is not to be. The landlady asks for money to pay the rent for the room. The stranger says that he has no money and slams the door in the landlady's face. The outraged landlady calls the police to have her unwelcome boarder evicted.

In a short time, the police constable arrives. He goes up to the room followed by a crowd of curious villagers. The constable knocks and the door is opened. The bandaged man begs them all to leave, but the crowd hoots him down.

The stranger is desperate. "You're crazy to know who I am, aren't you?" he cries through the gauze covering his mouth. "All right, I'll show you!"

The stranger reaches for the shield over his nose, yanks

1

it off, and hurls it at the villagers. "There's a souvenir for you!" he screams.

Next, his gloved hand removes the dark glasses. But there are no eyes to be seen, only two black holes. He begins to unwrap the bandages from around his face. They reveal nothing but empty space. "Look, he's all eaten away," says the constable.

Finally, the stranger slips out of his clothing, revealing that he is invisible. Wearing only a white shirt that seems to float in the air, the invisible man chases the villagers from the room.

This scene is from the movie *The Invisible Man* (Universal, 1933). The movie is based on a book, published in 1897, by the master science fiction writer, H. G. Wells. In the movie, the actor Claude Rains plays Jack Griffin, the invisible man. We hear the actor's voice but do not see him for most of the film. At most, we see what looks like an empty shirt, an empty dressing gown, or some other piece of clothing.

We learn that Griffin has become invisible by accident. Griffin was a scientist who had been experimenting on animals with a new drug. The animals became invisible. But the drug had an unfortunate side effect. It drove the animals mad.

Griffin still decided to try the drug on himself. The drug turned him invisible. But Griffin did not know how to reverse its effects. He could not discover how to become visible again.

Griffin decided to leave the laboratory so that no one would find out his secret. He had come to the village to hide, while he continued his efforts to become visible. But the drug had driven Griffin into madness.

"It came to me suddenly," said Griffin. "The drugs I

took seemed to light up my brain. Suddenly, I realized the power I held—the power to rule, to make the world grovel at my feet. Ha, ha. We'll soon put the world right now. We'll begin with a reign of terror. A few murders, here and there."

Griffin, now completely insane, attempts to wreck a train, rob a bank, and kill those in his way. For a time, it seems that he cannot be stopped. But a snowstorm forces him to take shelter in a barn. The police are alerted and surround the barn. They decide to drive Griffin out by setting fire to the barn.

Griffin bursts out of the barn, confident that his invisibility will help him to escape. But his footprints appear in the snow. The police shoot at the footprints and hit their unseen target.

The face of Griffin is seen only once, in the final scene of the movie. Only when Griffin is dead does he slowly turn visible. At first only a skull appears, then muscles, until finally we see his lifeless face.

This old movie is still enjoyable. The acting is excellent, the story is exciting, and there are some very funny scenes, particularly with the villagers at the beginning. Most of all, the special effects showing pieces of empty clothing moving around are believable and fun to watch.

The Invisible Man was such a success that it was followed by many other "invisible" movies. *The Invisible Man Returns* (Universal, 1940) starred the young actor Vincent Price. Price later became famous for his roles in many horror movies.

In *The Invisible Man Returns,* Price portrays Geoffrey Radcliff, an innocent man accused of killing his brother. Radcliff is given the drug of invisibility by Frank Griffin, the brother of the original invisible man. Radcliff escapes from the police and attempts to find the real murderer. But time is growing short, and the drug will soon begin to drive Radcliff mad.

Radcliff finally finds the killer and corners him in a coal mine. Radcliff is shot by the police but struggles on. Meanwhile, the real killer accidentally plunges to his death. Just before he dies, the killer confesses.

Radcliff manages to stagger into a hospital. He gets a blood transfusion from his girl friend, which peps him up and also makes him visible. The movie isn't bad, but not nearly as good as the original.

Other invisible people appeared (and disappeared) in *The Invisible Woman* (Universal, 1941), *The Invisible Agent* (Universal, 1942), and *The Invisible Man's Revenge* (Universal, 1944). None of these are great but all contain something of interest.

The Invisible Woman starred John Barrymore, once a very famous stage and screen actor. Barrymore was near the end of his career when he played in this movie. He acts the part of an odd scientist who turns Kitty Carroll, a fashion model, invisible.

The invisible woman returns to the department store in which she worked. She appears in a fashion show without her head and arms and frightens away the customers. She keeps changing from being invisible back to being visible at the most embarrassing times. Finally, Kitty and the scientist get married and have a child—who promptly fades away and becomes invisible.

The Invisible Agent was a spy movie made during World War II. Jon Hall plays Frank Raymond, the grandson of the original invisible man (he had changed his name). He uses what is left of his father's drug to make himself invisible. He parachutes behind enemy lines in Germany and

The Invisible Man Returns,
1940.
Courtesy of Universal.

The Invisible Man's Revenge,
1944.
Courtesy of Screen Gems.

steals a list of Nazi and Japanese spies in America. Peter Lorre, an old hand at horror movies, plays a villainous Japanese spy called Ikito who is trying to catch Raymond.

Most of the movie is very silly, but Lorre is very good. So are the special effects, such as when the invisible agent is caught in a fish net set with hundreds of fish hooks. Raymond finally escapes from Germany, leaving Ikito to commit hara-kiri in disgrace.

The *Invisible Man's Revenge* was a poor film that also had nothing to do with the characters in the original book. In *Revenge,* an escaped criminal forces a scientist to turn him invisible. The invisible criminal goes around killing his old enemies. He also needs blood to remain invisible and tries to get some from the scientist and the hero. The criminal finally comes to a bad end, when he is destroyed by an angry invisible dog named Brutus.

There were many more movies with the word *invisible* in their titles. In fact, there were dozens made even before *The Invisible Man* in 1933. Most of these were comedies, thrillers, or serials that featured someone who became invisible. Some of the later movies, such as *The Invisible Boy* (Metro-Goldwyn-Mayer, 1957) and the *Invisible Invaders* (United Artists, 1959), featured invisible creatures from outer space.

The comedians Abbott and Costello even got into the "invisible" act in *Abbott and Costello Meet the Invisible Man* (Universal-International, 1951). Some of the comedy scenes are quite funny. One scene shows a poker game played with an invisible man. The cards seem to float in the air. In another scene, the invisible man becomes drunk in a restaurant and starts to bother the patrons who naturally blame poor Lou Costello, who they think is responsible.

The funniest scene takes place in a prizefight ring. Cos-

The Invisible Boy, 1957. Courtesy of Metro-Goldwyn-Mayer.

tello is a prizefighter and Abbott is his manager. Costello's opponent seems sure to beat him up, but the invisible man is also in the ring. He keeps hitting away and helping Lou, whose fists never seem to make contact. It turns out to be a great way to win a fight.

Television also had its share of invisible people. *The Invisible Man* was an English TV series that had an American run in 1958 on CBS. It featured the adventures of Dr. Peter Brady, a young scientist whose experiments made him invisible. Fighting off evil forces, Brady used his invisibility to help mankind. Some fine English actors appeared in guest spots on the show. But interestingly enough, Brady was never shown, and the person whose voice was used was never given credit for his invisible role.

Still another series entitled *The Invisible Man* was on NBC in 1975. It featured David McCallum as Dr. Daniel Weston, a new invisible hero. In this series, McCallum was supposed to have a lifelike mask (actually, his real face) that he wore whenever he wanted to look visible. McCallum fought bad guys all over the world for just one season on TV. But it seems just a matter of time until we will see a new movie or TV show about an invisible person.

2. Dr. Jekyll and Mr. Hyde

One of the most frequently filmed stories of all times is Robert Louis Stevenson's *The Strange Case of Dr. Jekyll and Mr. Hyde* (1886). The story is about a good man, Dr. Jekyll, a scientist who has a savage personality hidden within him, the evil Mr. Hyde. Nowadays, when a person changes from being good to being evil, someone may say that he is like "Jekyll and Hyde."

The story tells how Dr. Jekyll had discovered a strange mixture of chemicals in his laboratory. The chemicals have changed Jekyll into the murderous Mr. Hyde, who tortures and kills people for pleasure. Here is how Stevenson describes what happens when Hyde tries to change back to Jekyll.

He put the glass [of potion] to his lips, and drank at one gulp. A cry followed; he reeled, staggered, clutched at the table, and held on . . . as I looked . . . he seemed to swell; his face became suddenly black, and the features seemed to melt and alter. . . .

"Oh, God!" I screamed, and "Oh, God" again and again; for there before my eyes—pale and shaken, and half fainting, and groping before him with his hands, like a man restored from death—there stood Henry Jekyll!

But even though Dr. Jekyll has taken over control of his body again, all is not well. It seems that once Jekyll has unleashed his evil side, it begins to overpower him. Mr. Hyde has become stronger and stronger as Jekyll has weakened. Finally, the drug is no longer needed to bring about the change. Dr. Jekyll simply goes to sleep at night and awakens as Mr. Hyde.

Dr. Jekyll cannot stand the agony of changing to Hyde any longer. A few minutes before Hyde is to return, claiming his body forever, Dr. Jekyll writes down his full confession. He swallows poison, thus destroying a monster by giving up his own life.

The book was a great success from the start. In a year's time it was performed as a stage play. By 1908, Dr. Jekyll had been made into a silent film. Many other silent film versions of the story were made in the years to follow. In 1920 alone, five movies based on Stevenson's story were released.

The best of all the silent versions was the 1920 Paramount production that featured the great stage actor John Barrymore. In the movie, we see Barrymore standing alone in his laboratory as Dr. Jekyll. He holds a strange drug in his hands. Suddenly, he drinks. His body jerks around and his face twists with pain. Finally, an evil leer changes his appearance. Before our eyes, Barrymore changes from the nice-looking Dr. Jekyll into the hideous Mr. Hyde. Barrymore showed the change by his acting, without the benefit of any trick photography.

In the rest of the movie, Barrymore does wear special Hyde makeup on his face and hands. They make him appear like a human-sized spider, with a pointed head and clawlike fingers.

Twelve years after Paramount made its silent film version, they made a new *Dr. Jekyll and Mr. Hyde* (1931). The remake had sound and featured a wonderful performance by the actor Fredric March in the double role of Jekyll and Hyde. March won that year's Academy Award for Best Actor for his performance in the movie.

9

For the great change scene, Jekyll played by March sees his image in a mirror. Slowly his face begins to line and darken. The background noise is the magnified beating of a human heart. The half-changed Jekyll drops behind a laboratory table. When he arises, he again looks into the mirror. His image is now that of a gorilla with oversized fangs.

The rest of the film is about the same as in the book, except for the character of Hyde. In the original story, Hyde was always somewhat human. But in this film, Hyde is much more of a monster. He looks like some great ape and kills without reason or mercy.

In the final scene in the movie, Hyde is chased by the police through his laboratory. He climbs upon a shelf and prepares to leap upon his pursuers. But a policeman's

Dr. Jekyll and Mr. Hyde, 1931. Courtesy of Paramount.

bullet brings him crashing to the ground. On the floor, Hyde changes back into Jekyll and dies.

Only nine more years passed before another film studio decided to make the movie once again. This *Dr. Jekyll and Mr. Hyde* (Metro-Goldwyn-Mayer, 1941) featured Spencer Tracy in the title roles. In this movie, there is little difference between Jekyll's and Hyde's facial appearance. The plot is about the same as in the earlier movie. Again Hyde dies at the end, changing back into Jekyll in a final close-up.

Columbia also made a sequel to the original with a film called *The Son of Dr. Jekyll* (1951). As you might expect, the son of Dr. Jekyll rediscovers the formula for the drug and uses it on himself. But he only uses it to show the police what had happened to his father. It is Jekyll's old associate, Dr. Lanyon, who is really using the drug and committing crimes. After a final battle between Jekyll's son and Dr. Lanyon, the laboratory burns down and Lanyon meets his death.

During the time that all these movies were being made, many other versions of the story were being filmed. Some of these were comedy takeoffs on the story. For example, in 1925, the comedian Stan Laurel (who later became part of the team of Laurel and Hardy) was featured in a movie called *Dr. Pyckle and Mr. Pride* (Standard Cinema Corporation). Mr. Pride, as played by Laurel, dashed through the streets tweaking noses and kicking people in the pants. He was hardly an evil man, only very mischievous.

Almost thirty years later, the comedians Bud Abbott and Lou Costello appeared in *Abbott and Costello Meet Dr. Jekyll and Mr. Hyde* (Universal-International, 1953). In this version, Boris Karloff, a veteran of horror films, played the roles of Jekyll and Hyde. Abbott and Costello played a pair

Abbott and Costello Meet Dr. Jekyll and Mr. Hyde,
1953. Courtesy of Universal-International.

of American detectives, Slim and Tubby, studying in London in the early 1900s.

One of the funnier scenes in the movie is when Tubby accidentally falls on a hypodermic loaded with Jekyll's drug. He promptly changes into a fat version of Mr. Hyde. The tubby Mr. Hyde is chased all over London by Slim and the police while the real Mr. Hyde escapes to his laboratory.

The real Hyde is finally cornered and falls to his death. Before Tubby regains his normal appearance, he bites a few policemen, all of whom become Hydelike monsters. The movie ends with the Hyde monsters chasing Slim and Tubby.

Jerry Lewis starred in still another comedy version of the Stevenson tale. In *The Nutty Professor* (Paramount, 1963), Lewis plays professor Julius Kelp, a bucktoothed teacher of chemistry to whom nobody pays much attention, particularly a girl Kelp likes. Kelp invents a chemical drink that

The Nutty Professor, 1963. Courtesy of Paramount.

changes him into a dark creature who slips out of the laboratory.

This "monster" turns out to be Buddy Love, a handsome and naughty playboy. In a funny twist of the story, Love (Hyde) looks more normal than Kelp (Jekyll). At the end of the movie, Love disappears leaving Kelp to get the girl.

Television discovered Jekyll and Hyde during the 1950s. Basil Rathbone (who portrayed Sherlock Holmes in many movies) starred in *Dr. Jekyll and Mr. Hyde* on the CBS series *Suspense* in 1951. Four years later, Michael Rennie played the roles on the *Climax* series.

A two-and-a-half hour special entitled *The Strange Case of Dr. Jekyll and Mr. Hyde* was made by the Canadian Broadcasting Company in 1967. It was shown the following year over the ABC television network. Movie villain Jack Palance played the roles in this production.

NBC aired a ninety-minute version of *Dr. Jekyll and Mr. Hyde* in 1973. Filmed in London, the show starred Kirk Douglas as Jekyll and Hyde. Very odd was the fact that this production was a musical. Imagine scenes such as Jekyll and his girl friend singing a duet in a cemetery! Somehow it all worked as Douglas snarled and sang his way through the show.

These movies and TV shows are just a few of the many ways that Stevenson's story has been used. There have been countless radio programs, records, and even comic books on the Jekyll and Hyde idea. It would be safe to say that we have not yet seen or heard the last version of *The Strange Case of Dr. Jekyll and Mr. Hyde.*

3. Mad Scientists and Weird Doctors

The Cabinet of Dr. Caligari (Decla. 1920) was one of the earliest movies that featured a mad doctor with strange powers. The best things about this silent film are the strange, eerie backgrounds of painted shadows, streets, and street lamps that look as if they were dreamt up by a madman.

The plot is very confused and difficult to follow. The story is set in a town in Germany that is being visited by a carnival. Dr. Caligari and his living zombie, Cesare, are in the carnival.

Cesare forecasts that Alan, a young student, will die by the next morning. When Alan is found murdered, his friend Francis alerts the police. They give chase to the doctor.

Caligari flees to a lunatic asylum where, it turns out, he is the director. Francis pursues him and discovers that "Caligari" was a hypnotist who lived a century ago. He also finds that Cesare has collapsed and died as a result of the director's mistreatment. The director has gone insane and become Caligari in his own mind. Francis tells the police and the director is taken away in a straitjacket.

But there is more to come. In the last scene of the movie, Francis himself is shown to be a mental patient in Director Caligari's lunatic asylum. He has been telling the Caligari story to another patient. So the entire story turns out to be the crazy dream of a madman.

Caligari is still an interesting movie to watch. It was one of the first movies to use strange low camera angles to

The Cabinet of Dr. Caligari, 1920. Courtesy of Decla.

make things appear huge and scary. Most of the scenes are dark and shadowy. After *Caligari,* many other horror movies began to use the same kind of camera tricks, weird backgrounds, and mad doctors.

Boris Karloff was an actor who often played mad doctors and crazy scientists in his long movie career. His best known role, however, was as the original Frankenstein's monster. In *The Man Who Lived Again* (Gaumont, 1936), Karloff plays a mad doctor who finds a way to transplant the brain of one person into another. As usual, that kind of messy work gets him into trouble, and he comes to a bad end.

Karloff struck again as a crazy scientist in *The Invisible Ray* (Universal, 1936). You'll never guess who plays his best friend in the movie. Give up? It's Bela Lugosi, best known for his portrayal of Count Dracula.

It seems that Karloff has discovered a substance called Radium X and becomes infected by its radiation. He is able to kill at a touch and project death rays from his eyes.

Leaving dayglow prints on the bodies of his victims, Karloff brings terror to the people who laughed at his discoveries. Even his faithful friend Lugosi is killed by his deadly touch. But again, Karloff comes to a bad end when the drugs that keep him alive are destroyed.

Some of the scenes in *The Invisible Ray* are quite good. For example, Karloff uses his high-powered glance to crumble one church statue for each of his victims. And one of the lines in the movie has become quite well known: "There are some things Man is not meant to know."

Karloff played still another mad scientist in *The Man They Could Not Hang* (Columbia, 1939). In this movie, he is first shown as the kindly inventor of a mechanical heart. But he earns a death sentence for murder because of a failed ex-

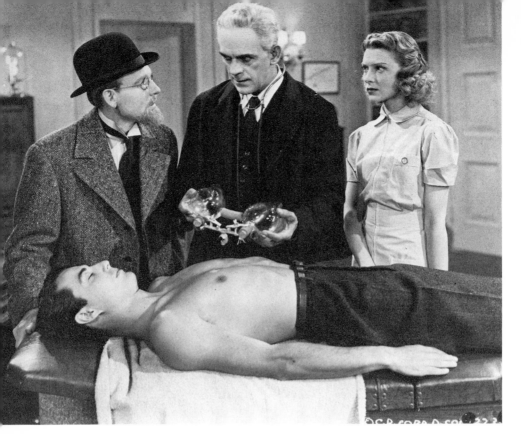

The Man They Could
Not Hang, 1939.
Courtesy of Columbia.

The Return of the Fly,
1959.
Courtesy of 20th
Century-Fox.

periment. He returns from the electric chair thanks to his own invention—the mechanical heart.

Now seeking to avenge himself, Karloff lures the judge and jury to a booby-trapped house. One victim after another is killed by the traps. But just before the last juror falls, Karloff is shot and killed—this time for good.

Vincent Price is another actor who has appeared in more than his share of crazy scientist movies. One of the best (and scariest) was *The Fly* (20th Century-Fox, 1958). Price plays the brother of a scientist, Al Hedison, who has discovered a way of sending animals from a booth in one location to another by taking apart and then rearranging their atoms. His invention works perfectly with guinea pigs and other laboratory animals.

But one day Hedison tries the experiment on himself. There is a teeny bit of an accident. A fly accidentally gets into the booth with Hedison. When Hedison arrives at his destination, he has his own body but the head and one claw of the fly. The fly winds up with Hedison's head and one human hand.

In order to sort things out, Hedison has to find the fly and repeat the experiment exactly. Unfortunately, they do not succeed. The fly is caught in a spider's web and dies screaming. Hedison meets an equally horrible fate in this movie (he has his head crushed in a vise), which is guaranteed to give anyone nightmares.

Price is back again in the same role in *The Return of the Fly* (20th Century-Fox, 1959). This movie begins where *The Fly* leaves off. Hedison's son decides to continue his father's work. Just like his dad, the son winds up with the head of a fly. This time, though, Price is able to track down the human fly.

In *The Abominable Dr. Phibes* (American International Pictures, 1971), Price plays a scientist, Dr. Phibes. Phibes becomes crazy when he loses his face in an automobile accident while rushing to his sick wife's bedside. But Phibes's wife has died during an operation. Phibes goes into hiding vowing revenge on the doctors who operated.

And what a revenge Phibes dreams up! He gets rid of his victims with plagues of rats, locusts, frogs, and boils. Finally, Phibes gets to the chief surgeon, played by actor Joseph Cotton. Phibes straps Cotton's son to an operating table, with the keys to his bonds sewn inside the boy's chest. Unless the boy is operated upon and freed from his bonds with the keys, he will be washed down with a bath of acid. The boy is just freed in the nick of time and Phibes is foiled.

Phibes is down but not out. In *Dr. Phibes Rises Again* (American International Pictures, 1973), Price is back again playing the crazy scientist. But this time, Price plays the role strictly for laughs. Phibes decides to take his dead wife to Egypt to look for a lost river of life. There Phibes finds a competing expedition and tries to do away with them. Price is aided in this movie by the comedians Terry-Thomas and Hugh Griffith. He needs all the help he can get, because this sequel is not nearly as good as the original.

Mad doctors and crazy scientists appear in so many films that it is impossible to mention them all. Here are just a few. In *The Colossus of New York* (Paramount, 1958), the brain of a scientist is transplanted by a misguided friend into the head of a large robot. The crazed robot sets out to destroy New York City. The dead scientist's son tries to stop the robot. New York City sleeps through the whole mess.

20

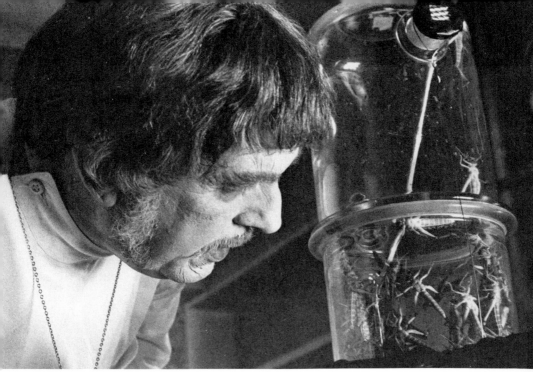

The Abominable Dr. Phibes,
1971.
Courtesy of American
International.

The Colossus of New York,
1958.
Courtesy of Paramount.

The Alligator People (20th Century-Fox, 1959) features a scientist who is experimenting with reptile parts. He gets a little mixed up in some of his experiments. So do some of his subjects. One turns into a kind of human alligator. The scientist tries to correct his little error, but his subject comes off looking worse than before. Well, what can a crazy scientist do after he says that he's sorry?

Sssssss (Universal, 1973) features still another scientist experimenting with reptiles. This one is a snake fancier. He sets about turning his daughter's boyfriend into a serpent. The daughter prefers her boyfriend the way he was. So will you. The film has some frightening moments and a good performance by Strother Martin as the evil scientist.

Not all movie scientists are evil, however. In *The Absent-Minded Professor* (Walt Disney, 1960), Fred MacMurray plays a scientist who invents a substance named flubber. Flubber makes things fly, such as cars. MacMurray even puts some flubber on the sneakers of basketball players. This allows them to drop the ball *down* into the basket. Can you imagine what basketball star Julius Erving could do with flubber. He would go into orbit!

4. Strange Children

Village of the Damned (Metro-Goldwyn-Mayer, 1960) is a movie filled with mounting suspense. The story begins in a small English village. One day, something strange happens. The phones stop working, radios produce nothing but static. No news comes in or out.

Other odd things occur. A plane flying over the village crashes in flames. A bus going to the village runs off the road before it can arrive. A postman coming to deliver mail falls off his bicycle and cannot continue.

The village lies silent and dark. All of the villagers fall unconscious. Even the animals stop all activity. Nothing stirs the whole day long.

At the end of the day, the villagers remember nothing when they awake. Everything seems to have come back to normal. Yet something has happened. Twelve women in the village are surprised to find out that they are going to have babies. Months later the women give birth all on the same day. Six blond-haired boys and six blond-haired girls are born.

Time passes and the twelve strange children are now of school age. They have set themselves apart from the other children in the village. They band together against the other villagers. Their cold stares can drive a person into danger and even death. No one has the power to stop them from doing what they want.

One of the children is the son of a scientist, played by George Sanders. Sanders is the only one in the village that the children respect and even partly trust. He becomes their teacher.

Sanders secretly believes that the children are dangerous to the people of the world. Yet how can the children be destroyed? They can read minds and force people to act against their will.

Sanders begins to practice hiding his thoughts from the children by thinking about other things. One day he arrives at their schoolhouse with a time bomb hidden in his briefcase. He attempts to conceal his knowledge of the bomb by thinking about a stone wall.

The children sense that something is wrong. They concentrate all their mental powers on Sanders's mind. Slowly they overpower his thoughts. They find out about the bomb, but it is too late. The bomb explodes, killing Sanders and the strange children.

Children of the Damned (Metro-Goldwyn-Mayer, 1964) was a good sequel to the earlier film. The story begins when scientists discover that six children with strange powers have been born in different countries. The governments of the countries begin to fear that the children will use their powers to take over the world.

But these children want only to be left in peace. Two scientists and an aunt of one of the children take their side against the governments. They bring the children together in London and try to reason with the government officials.

It is of no use. The six children make their last stand in a ruined cathedral in the middle of the city. They are surrounded by army units on all sides.

The world's leaders finally try to contact the defenseless children. They want to avoid bloodshed and reach some kind of understanding. But it is too late.

A soldier's careless hand hits a switch and gives the

Children of the Damned, 1964. Courtesy of Metro-Goldwyn-Mayer.

order for the guns to fire. In a few minutes, the cathedral is destroyed. The children die quietly without once having fought back.

The children were strange but they did no harm. They were killed because of the lack of understanding between different people and because of a military accident. The movie is not only exciting but it also makes you think about the way in which some wars begin.

These Are the Damned (Hammer, 1961) is also about

strange children. But the film has nothing to do with the others in this chapter. The story tells what happens to a group of children who have been deliberately exposed to radiation. The government performing the experiment hopes that the radiation will change the children so that they can survive an atomic war.

The children change but become radioactive themselves and dangerous to others. The government keeps the children prisoners in a hidden laboratory built beneath some sea cliffs. The children are cared for by people in protective radiation suits. They learn about the world by watching TV. They have never seen an adult human in person.

A few tourists accidentally find the laboratory and the children. The tourists are horrified at the experiment. They free the children who wander off along the sea cliffs.

The tourists decide to try to get help for the children. They leave in a speedboat as a government helicopter circles overhead. But the helicopter makes no attempt to stop their flight. The government knows that the tourists have been poisoned by the radioactive children. They will shortly die. The children wander around the caves crying for the help that will never come.

These Are the Damned has some good scenes and some interesting ideas. But so many things happen that it is difficult to make sense of what is going on.

It's Alive (Warner Brothers, 1974) is another film about a child with strange powers. The child's mother has taken some drugs that have an unforseen effect on her baby. The infant is much more powerful and intelligent than a normal human. It kills the doctors and nurses present at its birth and escapes from the hospital.

In the movie, you only catch short glimpses of the strange child. But they're enough. The thing has a bulging

26

It's Alive, 1974. Courtesy of Warner Brothers.

head and is all claws and teeth. It's also very fast and can run like a deer. In the final scenes, the deadly child is hunted down in the sewers of Los Angeles.

Children with strange powers are seen on TV from time to time. One of the stories on the science fiction series *The Outer Limits* was entitled "The Children of Spider County." In the story, five young geniuses have vanished. It seems that their father, an alien from a distant world in space, has come back to claim them.

Another story in the series was entitled "The Special One." In that episode, an agent from the planet Xenon is teaching some intelligent children on the earth. He has a special project in mind for them—the conquest of their own planet.

The TV series *Twilight Zone* also had several episodes that featured children. In one episode, entitled "It's a Good Life," a young boy with mysterious, destructive powers holds a community terrified. In another titled "Mute," a child who was raised to communicate just by telepathy is taught how to talk.

What makes children so scary in these movies? Perhaps because we think that only adults are sometimes evil and powerful and do bad things to those around them. But we usually think of children as weak and innocent. When children are evil or powerful, our views of the world are turned upside-down. And that makes children with strange powers even more frightening than adults would be.

5. Growing and Shrinking

The idea of growing or shrinking in size has long interested people. There are many fairy tales and myths that tell of people who grew to become giants or shrank to become doll-sized.

H. G. Wells, the author of *The Invisible Man* and many other great science fiction stories, wrote *The Food of the Gods* in 1903. It told of the invention of a special food that causes humans to grow into giants.

Insects and rats accidentally also eat the food and become giantlike. But the conflict between the giant humans and normal-sized people is the main point of the story.

Food of the Gods was used as the title for a movie made in 1976 (American International Pictures). The movie doesn't have much to do with Wells's original story. The movie is set on an island off the coast of British Columbia. A mysterious chemical oozing out of the ground is causing the local animals to grow very large.

A group of people become trapped in a farmhouse by a pack of giant wild rats. They are finally saved when the hero dynamites a local dam and floods the area. The special effects in the movie were good, but the dialogue was silly and the acting (except for the rats) was awful.

Bert I. Gordon, the producer and director of *Food of the Gods,* some twenty years earlier had made a movie about a person growing to become a giant. *The Amazing Colossal Man* (American International Pictures, 1957) was a low-budget film with poor special effects and a familiar story.

The Amazing Colossal Man, 1957. Courtesy of American International.

In the film, an army officer is caught in an atomic explosion that causes him to grow to the size of a human King Kong. The big guy is troubled by a weak heart that can't keep up with his body. He soon goes insane and starts destroying everything around him, including what seem to be cardboard buildings, before being destroyed himself.

The same year also saw the release of another terrible picture about giant-sized things, *The Beginning of the End* (Republic, 1957). In this movie, radioactive substances are put into the soil to make crops grow larger. They have some unexpected effects such as producing giant-sized grasshoppers and other insects.

THEM!, 1954. Courtesy of Warner Brothers.

A horde of these huge creepy-crawlers decide to eat Chicago. The Illinois National Guard is on hand to defend the city, but their bullets are not of much use. It's up to the scientist–hero to save the city. He serenades the insects with some high-pitched sounds and lures them to their destruction.

Much better than these movies was an earlier film about giant insects called *THEM!* (Warner Brothers, 1954). The film begins with two New Mexico highway patrolmen finding an overturned house trailer in the middle of the desert. The only person they find is a small girl who says the word *them* over and over again. A strange whistling sound is heard in the air.

Later that day the strange sound is heard again. The village general store is found destroyed and covered with a thin trail of sugar. One patrolman vanishes while investigating the scene, leaving behind only his bloodstained cap.

After several more strange happenings, the police, aided by a scientist, find a horde of giant ants in huge tunnels in the middle of the desert. It seems that the ants grew large as a result of atomic testing in the area.

The army bombs the inside of the insect city with poisonous gas. Though hundreds of the ants are killed, a queen ant and a mate escape in the direction of Los Angeles. There she lays her eggs in the city's sewer system. Soon the huge insects are again causing all kinds of trouble. They are finally discovered and the army storms in with flamethrowers.

THEM! features good acting, an interesting story, and fine special effects. The studio made several full-sized models of the giant ants. These were featured in close-ups with the human actors and look quite realistic.

If giant-sized animals are scary, can pint-sized human beings also be scary? The answer, as provided by the movie *The Devil Doll* (Metro-Goldwyn-Mayer, 1936), is yes. The movie stars the great actor Lionel Barrymore (brother of John Barrymore mentioned on pp. 4, 9). He plays a man wrongly convicted of a crime and sent to prison on Devil's Island. Barrymore escapes from the prison with another prisoner, an old man. The senior citizen turns out to be a scientist who has discovered a way to shrink living things.

Barrymore steals the invention and plans to use it for his revenge. He returns to his home and disguises himself as an old lady toymaker. He then sends what appear to be dolls to his enemies. The dolls are actually tiny humans in a trance. In the middle of the night they come to life and attack.

One of the dolls is shown being cuddled by a little girl. The doll gets away from the girl and carries out its deadly mission. It climbs up a bed to stab its victim with a poisoned needle. The other doll is tied in place with a huge bow on a Christmas tree. At night, it comes to life and goes on the attack. The movie is marvelously scary and the effects are good for their time.

Doctor Cyclops (Paramount, 1940) also featured human beings reduced in size. Doctor Thorkel (played by Albert Dekker) lures a group of scientists to his laboratory in Peru. Thorkel is bald, bullet-headed, and wears a pair of thick eyeglasses—the very image of how an evil scientist should look, at least according to Hollywood. Thorkel soon proves himself to be a bad guy when he shrinks his visitors down to doll size.

The little people escape but find themselves in a world full of danger—a cat that thinks that they would make a good meal, a huge chicken that takes a peck at them, a rainstorm that threatens to drown them, and other assorted horrors. Thorkel also goes after the shrunken scientists, shoots one, and tries to burn the others.

Believing that the little people are dead, Thorkel goes back to his cabin. But three survivors come after him. First they try to shoot the evil doctor with his own shotgun, but fail. Next they smash Thorkel's thick glasses, without which he is almost blind. Finally, they lure the furious doctor to an open mine shaft, where he falls to his death.

The name *Cyclops* comes from the name of the one-eyed giant in the Greek myth of Ulysses. Cyclops, like Doctor Thorkel, is made blind so that his prisoners can escape.

Doctor Cyclops was the first science fiction film to be made in color. The acting and special effects were quite good for the time, and the film is still enjoyable to watch.

Even better than *Doctor Cyclops* is *The Incredible Shrinking Man* (Universal-International, 1957). Scott Carey, the hero of the movie, played by actor Grant Williams, passes through a radioactive cloud. This causes him to shrink, slowly at first, but then faster and faster.

Carey tries to adjust to his shrinking along the way. Believing that he has stopped shrinking when he's three feet tall, he makes friends with a midget girl that he meets in a park.

But Carey keeps getting smaller and smaller, until he is

The Incredible Shrinking Man, 1957. Courtesy of Universal-International.

Fantastic Voyage, 1966. Courtesy of 20th Century-Fox.

reduced to living in a dollhouse. A cat attacks the dollhouse and attempts to eat him. The ant-sized Carey escapes to the cellar of the house. There he battles a huge spider and is nearly drowned by a leak in the house's boiler.

Carey finally overcomes these threats but still continues to shrink. Finally, we see him passing through a wire screen in a cellar window to go into the garden. We never find out what happens to Carey, but as he disappears he says: "To God there is no zero. I still exist." The film has a good

script, good special effects, and good acting, especially by Williams in the title role.

Even smaller than Carey is the five person crew in the movie *Fantastic Voyage* (20th Century-Fox, 1966). Four men and a woman, along with their submarine, are shrunk to microscopic size. The sub and its crew are injected into a person's bloodstream. Their mission is to perform a dangerous operation in the person's brain—from inside.

The tiny voyagers face many dangers within the body. They are also racing against time. They must perform the operation and get out of the body quickly. Otherwise, they will expand and grow to normal size while still inside.

The scenes of the inside of a body are truly fantastic. Richard Fleischer, the director of the film, ordered an enormous working model of the heart to be built. The heart was forty feet high and thirty feet wide and all of it moved. The brain is also very dramatic. It looks like a giant spiderweb pulsing with electrical flashes.

The crew featured Stephen Boyd as the brave captain, Donald Pleasance as the sweaty villain, and Raquel Welch as the beautiful lady scientist. But the real stars of the film are the great sets. See the movie the next time it shows up on TV. You'll enjoy it.

Not so enjoyable was a TV series called *World of Giants* (1959). This short-lived series used the props and sets left over from *The Incredible Shrinking Man.* The story followed the adventures of a six-inch-tall hero working as a spy for the government. Unfortunately, not only was the hero little, but so was the interest of most viewers.

Fantastic Voyage, 1966. Courtesy of 20th Century-Fox.

6. Mysterious Powers

The idea of living forever may seem to be attractive, but that's not the way it works out in the movies. *The Man in Half Moon Street* (Paramount, 1944) is the chilling story of a century-old doctor who doesn't look his age. It seems that he will remain immortal as long as he replaces a vital organ in his body every few years. Unfortunately, the organs come from murdered victims. Fortunately, Scotland Yard finally tracks the old-timer down and he is killed.

The same story was remade a few years later as *The Man Who Could Cheat Death* (Paramount, 1959). Anton Diffring played the evil doctor. This scary film also featured the actor Christopher Lee in an unusual role. Christopher Lee has played Dracula and other assorted villains in a host of movies. But he actually played the hero in *The Man Who Could Cheat Death.*

A different kind of immortal was shown in *The Picture of Dorian Gray* (Metro-Goldwyn-Mayer, 1945). The movie tells the story of an evil man who remains youthful and does not age. But a painting of the man kept in a locked room is gradually changing into a true picture of an aged monster. At the end, the painting and the man return to their true states. The movie features good performances by actors Hurd Hatfield, George Sanders, Angela Lansbury, and Peter Lawford.

A man who could live forever was the hero of a TV movie called *The Immortal* (ABC, 1969). Ben Richards, a test driver, has an accident. In the hospital, he discovers that

The Man Who Could Cheat Death, 1959. Courtesy of Paramount.

The Picture of Dorian Gray, 1945. Courtesy of Metro-Goldwyn-Mayer.

4D Man, 1959.
Courtesy of Screen Gems.

The Man with X-Ray Eyes, 1963.
Courtesy of American International.

his strange blood type makes him immune to disease and to aging. Ben is forced to flee when a rich oldster tries to make him a captive blood donor.

The next year, *The Immortal* became a weekly series. Each week Ben donated his blood to deserving people and fled from the rich villain. The series was much shorter-lived than Ben. It lasted for only one year.

Besides immortality, movies told of people with many other kinds of strange powers. The hero of *Atomic Man* (Allied Artists, 1956) is a scientist who has been dosed with atomic radiation. This has affected him in a peculiar way. He is slightly out of time with the present. To be exact, he is seven seconds in the future. That means he reacts to things just before they occur. The idea is interesting, but the movie doesn't really develop it to any great extent.

Another scientist is the hero of *4D Man* (United Artists, 1959). Robert Lansing stars as the scientist who discovers how to go into a fourth dimension. This allows him to pass through solid things, such as walls. Eventually, this ability gets him into trouble when he starts to return to a normal state while walking through a wall. He changes. The wall doesn't. That's trouble.

Still another scientist is the hero of *The Man with X-Ray Eyes* (American International Pictures, 1963). Ray Milland plays the scientist who discovers a serum that allows a person to see through solids. Milland accidentally kills a fellow scientist and then tries to run from the police.

Milland first hides in a small-time carnival. There he uses his powers to see through things as an act in the sideshow. Milland's girl friend catches up with him after a while. They decide to go to Las Vegas to do a little gambling. They win a lot of money, but then they attract the attention of the police.

The police chase Milland into the desert, where he winds up in the tent of a crazy preacher. Milland's eyes have now become black holes. He stares into the air and tells the crowd in the tent that he can see into the center of the universe. There is a gory ending that doesn't help to make the movie any better. Nevertheless, Milland gives a good performance and the movie isn't that bad.

The scientists in *The Projected Man* (Universal, 1966) are working on a machine that will project matter across a distance. But one of their experiments goes slightly wrong. One of the scientists comes out of the machine with half his face gone and an electric touch in his hands. After killing a few people, the crazed scientist goes to a power station to get recharged. The police find the projected man there and he is short-circuited.

Strange powers of the mind come into play in *Donovan's Brain* (United Artists, 1953). An earlier version of the same story had been made under the title *The Lady and the Monster* (Republic, 1944).

The story begins when a scientist keeps alive the brain of evil Tom Donovan after Donovan's body dies in a plane crash. The brain begins to send out mental messages to the young scientist. Soon the brain takes over and controls the scientist's every action. Donovan's brain is seeking revenge upon some of his former business partners. Of course, it all ends badly for the brain, who can't think of anything to do when the end comes.

Brain power is also the subject of *The Power* (Metro-Goldwyn-Mayer, 1967). The story takes place in a science research institute. One of the scientists is using the vast powers of his mind to kill and to make others do as he wants. The hero, played by George Hamilton, sets out to find the villain. The ending is a mental showdown between

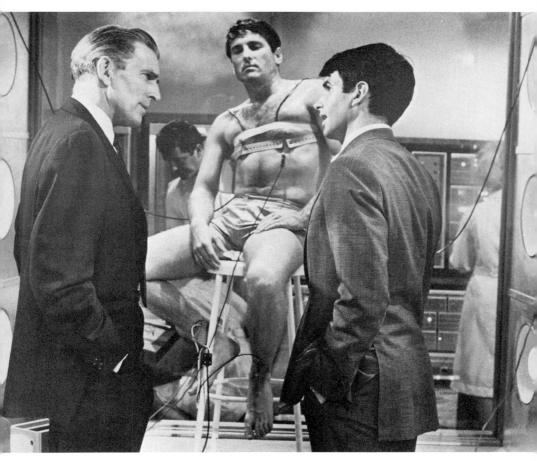

The Power, 1967. Courtesy of Metro-Goldwyn-Mayer.

Hamilton and the evil mastermind.

There are many, many science fiction books and stories about people with strange powers. Two of the best are *Odd John* (1935) by Olaf Stapledon and *Slan* (1940) by A. E. van Vogt. John is able to read minds and has super intelligence. Although John is well able to take over control of the world, he decides not to do so. "It would be like trying to civilize a pack of monkeys," he says.

Slan is about a race of people who can read minds and

who also have a double heart. They are stronger and more intelligent than humans. But there are only a few of them and they are being hunted down like wild beasts by normal humans. How these super people survive through their telepathic powers and come to terms with the rest of humanity makes for an exciting and thoughtful story.

Comic book super heroes have all kinds of strange powers. Superman, Wonderwoman, the Incredible Hulk, Spiderman, Captain Marvel, Batman and Robin, and the Human Torch are only a few of many. TV has produced some of its own super heroes with shows such as *The Six Million Dollar Man* and *The Bionic Woman.* There seems to be no end to the number of movies, TV shows, and books about people with mysterious powers.

7. Time Travelers

A Tale of the Ragged Mountains was written by Edgar Allan Poe in 1843. It is one of the earliest stories about a time traveler. The story begins with a man wandering around in the mountains of Virginia. He discovers that somehow he has been transported back to the year 1780. The story does not try to explain how or why this happened.

A very popular early story about a time traveler was Mark Twain's *Connecticut Yankee in King Arthur's Court* (1889). The hero somehow journeys into the past when he is hit on the head. He wakes to find himself in England at the time of King Arthur. He has all kinds of fun and adventures. He introduces modern plumbing, telephones, and bicycles to the olden times of King Arthur. The Yankee returns to the present by going to sleep. This leaves it up to the reader to decide whether the whole tale may have been only a dream.

Connecticut Yankee was made into a movie at least three times: in 1920, in 1931 with Will Rogers, and in 1949 with Bing Crosby. The story has also been used on the stage as a musical play with songs by Cole Porter.

Time travel really entered modern times with *The Time Machine* (1895) by H. G. Wells. Wells not only used a time machine in his story but also described how it felt to travel in the machine: "I am afraid I cannot convey the peculiar sensations of time travelling. They are excessively unpleasant. There is a feeling . . . of a helpless headlong motion.

A Connecticut Yankee in King Arthur's Court, 1948. Courtesy of Paramount.

As I put on pace, night followed day like the flapping of a black wing. . . ."

The time traveler starts out from the nineteenth century and winds up thousands and thousands of years in the future. The world has changed completely. There are only two groups of people left: a childlike people called the Eloi who spend all their time in games, eating, and drinking; and the monstrous Morlocks who live below the ground with their machines. The Morlocks seem to take care of the Eloi, but they are really breeding them for food the same way we breed cattle.

At the end of the book, the time traveler journeys even farther into the future. He sees the final fate of the earth

The Time Machine, 1960. Courtesy of Metro-Goldwyn-Mayer.

itself. The sun has slowly burnt itself out and the earth lies cold, frozen, and dead.

The Time Machine was made into a good movie in 1960 by Metro-Goldwyn-Mayer. Rod Taylor stars as the inventor who zooms into the future. Along the way, Taylor watches London being destroyed in an atomic war. He finishes up in the year 802,701, where he meets the Eloi and the Morlocks.

But unlike the hero of the book who only watches what happens, the movie's time traveler takes action. He fights the Morlocks and gets the Eloi to join in the battle. At the end, the Eloi live happily ever after (or so it seems).

Though the film made changes in Wells's original story, it had many good special effects by George Pal that make it enjoyable viewing. The machine is beautiful, all dials and spinning lights. The time-traveling scenes are particularly good. We see the laboratory clock move forward, candles melt, day and night pass by quickly. The Morlocks are also quite ugly and just right for their "bad guy" role.

H. G. Wells himself appears as a character in a recent movie about time travel called *Time After Time* (Warner Brothers, 1979). The story has Wells chasing Jack the Ripper from Victorian London into present-day California. At the end of the movie, Wells returns to his own time with a bride from the present. The movie is suspenseful and also has many funny scenes of Wells trying to figure out modern times.

Not nearly as good is *The Time Travelers* (American International Pictures, 1964). The film shows four scientists accidentally making a time door in their laboratory. They go through the door into a future world that is suffering the aftereffects of an atomic world. The scientists find that the remaining humans are battling with mutants created by

48

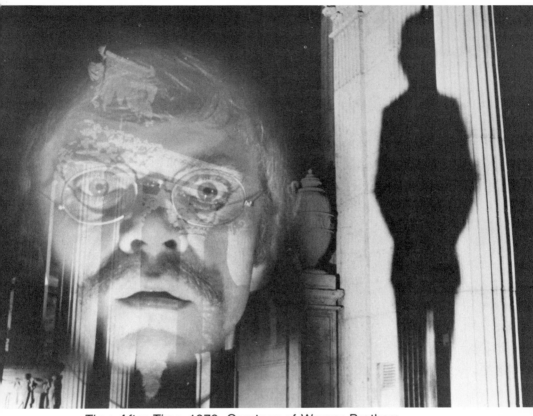

Time After Time, 1979. Courtesy of Warner Brothers.

the atomic radiation. Some of the special effects aren't bad, but most of the movie is just silly.

The big movie success of time-travel stories was *Planet of the Apes* (20th Century-Fox, 1968). The movie starred Charlton Heston as an astronaut whose spaceship goes through a time warp and winds up thousands of years in the future.

When Heston and his two living companions crash-land, they think that they are on some distant planet. To their surprise, they discover human inhabitants. But the humans are uncivilized and unable to talk. Soon the astronauts are even more surprised when the humans are surrounded by horse-riding gorillas that wear clothing, carry guns, and speak in English.

One of the astronauts is killed, another is hit on the head and mentally damaged, and Heston is wounded in the neck. Heston's neck injury leaves him unable to speak. He is taken prisoner by the gorillas and winds up in an ape laboratory.

Heston tries to communicate with two scientist chimps (played by Kim Hunter and Roddy McDowall). Finally, Heston is able to convince the chimps that he is an intelligent human by regaining his voice and speaking to them. Other ape scientists see the speaking human as a threat to ape society. They are going to have Heston killed, but the two chimps help him escape into the "forbidden zone." The film ends with Heston finding the half-destroyed Statue of Liberty. He then realizes that he is still on the earth (in some future time) and not on some distant world.

The film is very well made, with fine special effects, good acting, and some funny moments. But the story doesn't make much sense. For example, Heston doesn't realize till the very end that the ape planet is really a future earth— even though the apes speak English. Still, the film was so popular that there were four sequels.

The best of the sequels was the first, *Beneath the Planet of the Apes* (20th Century-Fox, 1969). Astronaut James Franciscus is looking for his old buddy, Charlton Heston, in the ruins of the earth. Things are even worse on the planet this time around. The apes rule the land above ground, while a group of scared humans live underground. Franciscus finds Heston, but by that time the apes and underground humans are at war. The film ends with a doomsday bomb exploding and the earth being totally destroyed.

50

Planet of the Apes, 1968. Courtesy of 20th Century-Fox.

The other sequels just became sillier and sillier. In 1974, CBS even had a series based on the film. The TV version of *Planet of the Apes* lasted for one season but was never as popular as the original movie.

Another TV series about time travelers was *The Time Tunnel* (ABC, 1967). The series, created and produced by Irwin Allen (who was responsible for *Land of the Giants, Lost In Space,* and other TV science fiction series), also lasted for only one year. The story featured two scientists that were lost in time. Each week they were transported into another time, usually in the middle of an important event in history but sometimes into the future. The special effects of the time tunnel itself were quite good, especially of the spiral tunnel that looked like a revolving kaleidoscope of "time fragments." But the stories were not always very interesting.

After so many movies, TV series, and books about people with strange powers, you might think that there are no more new ones being filmed or written. But that's not so. Imagination has no limits. And who knows what strange stories are even now awaiting their chance to thrill and amuse us in the future.

Beneath the Planet of the Apes, 1969. Courtesy of 20th Century-Fox.

Index